명언 & 문학 작품 필사로 영어 필기체가 저절로 손에 착!

100문장으로 끝내는
정말 쉬운 영어 필기체

시원스쿨닷컴

100문장으로 끝내는
정말 쉬운 영어 필기체

초판 1쇄 발행 2025년 10월 31일

지은이 시원스쿨어학연구소
펴낸곳 (주)에스제이더블유인터내셔널
펴낸이 양홍걸 이시원

홈페이지 www.siwonschool.com
주소 서울시 영등포구 영신로 166 시원스쿨
교재 구입 문의 02)2014-8151
고객센터 02)6409-0878

ISBN 979-11-7550-018-1 13740
Number 1-010202-30309900-06

이 책은 저작권법에 따라 보호받는 저작물이므로 무단복제와 무단전재를 금합니다. 이 책 내용의 전부 또는 일부를 이용하려면 반드시 저작권자와 ㈜에스제이더블유인터내셔널의 서면 동의를 받아야 합니다.

명언 & 문학 작품 필사로 영어 필기체가 저절로 손에 착!

100문장으로 끝내는
정말 쉬운 영어 필기체

온라인 워크시트 무료제공!
siwonschool.com

직장인부터 유학 준비생까지, 손글씨가 필요한
모두를 위한 영어 필기체 쓰기 노트

There is no substitute for hard work.
Fill your paper with the breathings of your heart.
Every failure is a step to success.
Practice makes perfect.
Lost time is never found again.

S 시원스쿨닷컴

이 책 쓰는 법

1   영어 필기체에 꼭 필요한 선긋기와 알파벳 이어쓰기로
영어 필기체 쓰기를 위한 준비를 하세요.

2   본격적으로 각 **알파벳이 들어간 단어들을 연습**합니다.
중학교 수준의 단어들로 구성되어 부담 없이 단어와
영어 필기체를 동시에 익힐 수 있습니다.

3   편지, 영어 일기 등 **쓰기에 필요한 주요 문장 100문장**을
연습해 보세요.

4   <오즈의 마법사> 속 명문장과 <이솝 우화>를
영어 필기체로 쓰면서 **고전 문학**을 함께 즐겨보세요.

5   영어 필기체를 활용하기에 좋은 **다양한 형태의 필기체**를
연습해 보고 자신감을 향상시키세요.

차례

1 `Warm-up` 선 긋기 연습 — 8

2 `Warm-up` 알파벳 써 보기 — 9

3 `Step 1` 단어 써 보기 — 10

4 `Bonus 1` 다양한 나라 이름 써 보기 — 38

5 `Bonus 2` 다양한 직업명 써 보기 — 40

6 `Bonus 3` 다양한 교통수단 이름 써 보기 — 42

7 `Step 2` 문장 써 보기 — 44

8 `Step 3` 문학작품 써 보기 — 76

9 `Bonus 4` 카드, 편지를 위한 예쁜 필기체 써 보기 — 94

대문자 미리보기

Capital Letter

A	B	C	D
E	F	G	H
I	J	K	L
M	N	O	P
Q	R	S	T
U	V	W	X
Y	Z		

소문자 미리보기

Small Letter

a	b	c	d
e	f	g	h
i	j	k	l
m	n	o	p
q	r	s	t
u	v	w	x
y	z		

Warm-up

선긋기 연습
필기체 쓰기에 필요한 선들을 충분히 연습하고 필기체를 쓸 준비를 하세요.

알파벳 이어쓰기

알파벳을 따로 써 보고 연결해서 익숙해지도록 충분히 연습해 보세요.

ABCDEFGHIJKLMNOPQRSTUVWXYZ

abcdefghijklmnopqrstuvwxyz

ABCDEFGHIJKLMNOPQRSTUVWXYZ

abcdefghijklmnopqrstuvwxyz

Opportunity knocks but once.

100문장으로 끝내는 정말 쉬운 영어 필기체

단어 써보기

 알파벳 A 쓰기

A a *a*

📝 **A가 맨 앞에 오는 단어를 연습해 보세요.**

advance
advance 전진

animal
animal 동물

answer
answer 답

📝 **A가 중간에 오는 단어를 연습해 보세요.**

language
language 언어

paper
paper 종이

table
table 테이블

📝 **A가 맨 뒤에 오는 단어를 연습해 보세요.**

area
area 지역

sofa
sofa 소파

formula
formula 공식

B ℬ b

알파벳 B 쓰기

📝 B가 맨 앞에 오는 단어를 연습해 보세요.

blue
blue 파란

bird
bird 새

baby
baby 아기

📝 B가 중간에 오는 단어를 연습해 보세요.

cable
cable 케이블

rabbit
rabbit 토끼

number
number 숫자

📝 B가 맨 뒤에 오는 단어를 연습해 보세요.

absorb
absorb 흡수하다

bulb
bulb 전구

club
club 클럽

알파벳 C 쓰기

C c

✏️ C가 **맨 앞**에 오는 단어를 연습해 보세요.

cat
cat 고양이

cup
cup 컵

city
city 도시

✏️ C가 **중간**에 오는 단어를 연습해 보세요.

ocean
ocean 바다

actor
actor 배우

picnic
picnic 소풍

✏️ C가 **맨 뒤**에 오는 단어를 연습해 보세요.

magic
magic 마법

specific
specific 구체적인

public
public 공공의

알파벳 D쓰기

D *D d*

✏️ D가 맨 앞에 오는 단어를 연습해 보세요.

decrease
decrease 감소하다

door
door 문

drop
drop 떨어지다

✏️ D가 중간에 오는 단어를 연습해 보세요.

garden
garden 정원

model
model 모델

order
order 주문하다

✏️ D가 맨 뒤에 오는 단어를 연습해 보세요.

bed
bed 침대

kid
kid 아이

food
food 음식

알파벳 E쓰기

✎ E가 **맨 앞**에 오는 단어를 연습해 보세요.

experience
experience 경험

ear
ear 귀

elephant
elephant 코끼리

✎ E가 **중간**에 오는 단어를 연습해 보세요.

secret
secret 비밀

meter
meter 미터

penne
penne 파스타

✎ E가 **맨 뒤**에 오는 단어를 연습해 보세요.

cake
cake 케이크

smile
smile 미소

phone
phone 전화

알파벳 F쓰기

F f

✏️ F가 맨 앞에 오는 단어를 연습해 보세요.

fish
fish 물고기

father
father 아버지

friend
friend 친구

✏️ F가 중간에 오는 단어를 연습해 보세요.

coffee
coffee 커피

office
office 사무실

buffet
buffet 뷔페

✏️ F가 맨 뒤에 오는 단어를 연습해 보세요.

chef
chef 셰프

leaf
leaf 잎

roof
roof 지붕

알파벳 G쓰기

G G g

📝 **G가 맨 앞**에 오는 단어를 연습해 보세요.

game
game 게임

girl
girl 소녀

grammar
grammar 문법

📝 **G가 중간**에 오는 단어를 연습해 보세요.

tiger
tiger 호랑이

begin
begin 시작하다

sugar
sugar 설탕

📝 **G가 맨 뒤**에 오는 단어를 연습해 보세요.

dog
dog 개

bag
bag 가방

egg
egg 달걀

H h

✏️ H가 맨 앞에 오는 단어를 연습해 보세요.

happy
happy 행복한

hesitate
hesitate 주저하다

house
house 집

✏️ H가 중간에 오는 단어를 연습해 보세요.

behind
behind 뒤에

photo
photo 사진

behave
behave 행동하다

✏️ H가 맨 뒤에 오는 단어를 연습해 보세요.

tooth
tooth 이

bath
bath 목욕

push
push 밀다

알파벳 I 쓰기

I l i

I가 맨 앞에 오는 단어를 연습해 보세요.

ice
ice 얼음

idea
idea 아이디어

invite
invite 초대하다

I가 중간에 오는 단어를 연습해 보세요.

citizen
citizen 시민

river
river 강

time
time 시간

I가 맨 뒤에 오는 단어를 연습해 보세요.

chili
chili 고추

sushi
sushi 스시

spaghetti
spaghetti 스파게티

📝 **J가 맨 앞에 오는 단어를 연습해 보세요.**

juice
juice 주스

jacket
jacket 자켓

job
job 일

📝 **J가 중간에 오는 단어를 연습해 보세요.**

adjoin
adjoin 인접하다

object
object 목적

project
project 프로젝트

영어 필기체 소문자를 이어서 써 보세요

abcdefghijklmnopqrstuvwxyz

알파벳 K 쓰기

K K k

✏️ **K가 맨 앞에 오는 단어를 연습해 보세요.**

king
king 왕

key
key 열쇠

keyboard
keyboard 키보드

✏️ **K가 중간에 오는 단어를 연습해 보세요.**

baker
baker 제빵사

ticket
ticket 표

monkey
monkey 원숭이

✏️ **K가 맨 뒤에 오는 단어를 연습해 보세요.**

book
book 책

desk
desk 책상

milk
milk 우유

L l

알파벳 L 쓰기

📝 **L이 맨 앞에 오는 단어를 연습해 보세요.**

lamp
lamp 램프

lip
lip 입술

lion
lion 사자

📝 **L이 중간에 오는 단어를 연습해 보세요.**

yellow
yellow 노란색

hello
hello 안녕

color
color 색

📝 **L이 맨 뒤에 오는 단어를 연습해 보세요.**

ball
ball 공

pool
pool 수영장

school
school 학교

알파벳 M쓰기

📝 **M이 맨 앞에 오는 단어를 연습해 보세요.**

measure
measure 측정하다

mind
mind 마음

mix
mix 섞다

📝 **M이 중간에 오는 단어를 연습해 보세요.**

lemon
lemon 레몬

summer
summer 여름

tomato
tomato 토마토

📝 **M이 맨 뒤에 오는 단어를 연습해 보세요.**

farm
farm 농장

team
team 팀

room
room 방

✏️ **N이 맨 앞에 오는 단어를 연습해 보세요.**

name
name 이름

nest
nest 둥지

night
night 밤

✏️ **N이 중간에 오는 단어를 연습해 보세요.**

dinner
dinner 저녁식사

planet
planet 행성

piano
piano 피아노

✏️ **N이 맨 뒤에 오는 단어를 연습해 보세요.**

moon
moon 달

man
man 남자

pen
pen 펜

O o

📝 **O가 맨 앞에 오는 단어를 연습해 보세요.**

one
one 하나

open
open 열다

owl
owl 부엉이

📝 **O가 중간에 오는 단어를 연습해 보세요.**

octopus
octopus 문어

robot
robot 로봇

story
story 이야기

📝 **O가 맨 뒤에 오는 단어를 연습해 보세요.**

mango
mango 망고

potato
potato 감자

solo
solo 단독의

📝 **P가 맨 앞에 오는 단어를 연습해 보세요.**

poster
poster 포스터

pitch
pitch 던지다

pineapple
pineapple 파인애플

📝 **P가 중간에 오는 단어를 연습해 보세요.**

apple
apple 사과

laptop
laptop 노트북

topic
topic 주제

📝 **P가 맨 뒤에 오는 단어를 연습해 보세요.**

map
map 지도

cap
cap 모자

shop
shop 가게

Q q

✎ Q가 맨 앞에 오는 단어를 연습해 보세요.

queen
queen 여왕

quote
quote 인용하다

question
question 질문

✎ Q가 중간에 오는 단어를 연습해 보세요.

aqua
aqua 물

equal
equal 같은

frequency
frequency 빈도

영어 필기체 소문자를 이어서 써 보세요.

abcdefghijklmnopqrstuvwxyz

알파벳 R쓰기

R
R

📝 **R이 맨 앞에 오는 단어를 연습해 보세요.**

red
red 빨강

red

rest
rest 나머지

rest

rich
rich 부유한

rich

📝 **R이 중간에 오는 단어를 연습해 보세요.**

green
green 초록색

green

orange
orange 오렌지

orange

carry
carry 나르다

carry

📝 **R이 맨 뒤에 오는 단어를 연습해 보세요.**

car
car 자동차

car

star
star 별

star

doctor
doctor 의사

doctor

알파벳 S쓰기

S

📝 **S가 맨 앞에 오는 단어를 연습해 보세요.**

sit
sit 앉다

sun
sun 태양

sky
sky 하늘

📝 **S가 중간에 오는 단어를 연습해 보세요.**

basket
basket 바구니

castle
castle 성

island
island 섬

📝 **S가 맨 뒤에 오는 단어를 연습해 보세요.**

bus
bus 버스

class
class 수업

glass
glass 유리

T *T t*

T가 맨 앞에 오는 단어를 연습해 보세요.

tent
tent 텐트

tease
tease 놀리다

trend
trend 동향

T가 중간에 오는 단어를 연습해 보세요.

water
water 물

hotel
hotel 호텔

letter
letter 편지

T가 맨 뒤에 오는 단어를 연습해 보세요.

hat
hat 모자

fruit
fruit 과일

front
front 앞면

알파벳 U 쓰기

U U u

✏️ U가 맨 앞에 오는 단어를 연습해 보세요.

umbrella
umbrella 우산

uncle
uncle 삼촌

unit
unit 단위

✏️ U가 중간에 오는 단어를 연습해 보세요.

music
music 음악

autumn
autumn 가을

tutor
tutor 가정교사

✏️ U가 맨 뒤에 오는 단어를 연습해 보세요.

you
you 너

tofu
tofu 두부

menu
menu 메뉴

V

✏️ V가 맨 앞에 오는 단어를 연습해 보세요.

violin
violin 바이올린

voice
voice 목소리

village
village 마을

✏️ V가 중간에 오는 단어를 연습해 보세요.

seven
seven 일곱

movie
movie 영화

travel
travel 여행

영어 필기체 소문자를 이어서 써 보세요.

abcdefghijklmnopqrstuvwxyz

W w

✏️ W가 맨 앞에 오는 단어를 연습해 보세요.

watch
watch 시계

way
way 방법

window
window 창문

✏️ W가 중간에 오는 단어를 연습해 보세요.

flower
flower 꽃

tower
tower 탑

power
power 힘

✏️ W가 맨 뒤에 오는 단어를 연습해 보세요.

cow
cow 소

snow
snow 눈

show
show 보여주다

알파벳 X쓰기

X가 **맨 앞**에 오는 단어를 연습해 보세요.

xenophobia
xenophobia 외국인 혐오

xerophthalmia
xerophthalmia 안구건조증

xylitol
xylitol 자일리톨

X가 **중간**에 오는 단어를 연습해 보세요.

taxi
taxi 택시

extra
extra 추가의

boxer
boxer 복서

X가 **맨 뒤**에 오는 단어를 연습해 보세요.

box
box 상자

six
six 여섯

relax
relax 쉬다

알파벳 Y 쓰기

Y y *Y y* *Y y*

📝 **Y가 맨 앞에 오는 단어를 연습해 보세요.**

yesterday
yesterday 어제

yield
yield 산출하다

young
young 젊은

📝 **Y가 중간에 오는 단어를 연습해 보세요.**

style
style 스타일

royal
royal 왕의

player
player 선수

📝 **Y가 맨 뒤에 오는 단어를 연습해 보세요.**

boy
boy 소년

toy
toy 장난감

day
day 하루/날

알파벳 Z쓰기

✏️ Z가 **맨 앞**에 오는 단어를 연습해 보세요.

zoo
zoo 동물원

zoom
zoom 급등하다

zebra
zebra 얼룩말

✏️ Z가 **중간**에 오는 단어를 연습해 보세요.

pizza
pizza 피자

crazy
crazy 미친

lazy
lazy 게으른

✏️ Z가 **맨 뒤**에 오는 단어를 연습해 보세요.

fizz
fizz 거품 소리

jazz
jazz 재즈

topaz
topaz 토파즈

다양한 나라 이름

세계 각국의 이름을 필기체로 써보며 연습해 보세요.

Turkey
Turkey 튀르키예

United Kingdom
United Kingdom 영국

Canada
Canada 캐나다

Australia
Australia 호주

New Zealand
New Zealand 뉴질랜드

France
France 프랑스

Germany
Germany 독일

Italy
Italy 이탈리아

Spain
Spain 스페인

Portugal
Portugal 포르투갈

Brazil 브라질

Mexico 멕시코

Argentina 아르헨티나

South Korea 대한민국

Japan 일본

China 중국

India 인도

Thailand 태국

Egypt 이집트

Poland 폴란드

다양한 직업

다양한 직업명을 필기체로 써 보며 연습해 보세요.

Pharmacist
Pharmacist 약사

Nurse
Nurse 간호사

Teacher
Teacher 교사, 선생님

Student
Student 학생

Engineer
Engineer 엔지니어, 기술자

Scientist
Scientist 과학자

Artist
Artist 예술가

Musician
Musician 음악가

Writer
Writer 작가, 글쓴이

Chef
Chef 요리사

Pilot
Pilot 비행기 조종사

Driver
Driver 운전사, 기사

Farmer
Farmer 농부

Therapist
Therapist 치료사

Firefighter
Firefighter 소방관

Soldier
Soldier 군인

Actor
Actor 배우

Singer
Singer 가수

Dancer
Dancer 춤추는 사람

Lawyer
Lawyer 변호사

다양한 교통수단

여러 교통수단의 이름을 필기체로 써 보며 연습해 보세요.

Car
Car 자동차

Bus
Bus 버스

Taxi
Taxi 택시

Subway
Subway 지하철

Train
Train 기차

Tram
Tram 노면전차

Bicycle
Bicycle 자전거

Motorcycle
Motorcycle 오토바이

Scooter
Scooter 스쿠터

Truck
Truck 트럭, 화물차

Van
Van 승합차

Ship
Ship 선박

Boat
Boat 보트

Ferry
Ferry 여객선

Airplane
Airplane 비행기

Helicopter
Helicopter 헬리콥터

Rickshaw
Rickshaw 인력거

Submarine
Submarine 잠수함

Carriage
Carriage 마차

Monorail
Monorail 모노레일

Nothing will work unless you do.

100문장으로 끝내는 정말 쉬운 영어 필기체

문장 써보기

생활 영어 필수 문장 20

음식 주문하기

1 *Can I have a coffee, please?*
Can I have a coffee, please? 커피 한 잔 주세요.

2 *I'd like a sandwich.*
I'd like a sandwich. 샌드위치 하나 주세요.

3 *Do you have any recommendations?*
Do you have any recommendations? 추천해 주실 만한 게 있나요?

4 *The food looks delicious.*
The food looks delicious. 음식이 맛있어 보여요.

길 찾을 때 필수 표현

5 *Excuse me, where is the bus stop?*

Excuse me, where is the bus stop? 실례합니다, 버스 정류장이 어디인가요?

Excuse me, where is the bus stop?

6 *How can I get to the station?*

How can I get to the station? 역에는 어떻게 가나요?

How can I get to the station?

7 *Is it far from here?*

Is it far from here? 여기서 멀어요?

Is it far from here?

8 *Can you show me on the map?*

Can you show me on the map? 지도에서 보여 주실 수 있나요?

Can you show me on the map?

몸 상태 표현하기

9

I don't feel well.

I don't feel well. 몸이 좋지 않아요.

I don't feel well.

10

I have a headache.

I have a headache. 머리가 아파요.

I have a headache.

11

Can I see a doctor?

Can I see a doctor? 의사를 볼 수 있을까요?

Can I see a doctor?

12

I feel better now.

I feel better now. 지금은 좀 나아졌어요.

I feel better now.

쇼핑할 때 필수 표현

13 *How much is this?*

How much is this? 이거 얼마예요?

How much is this?

14 *Can I try it on?*

Can I try it on? 입어 봐도 되나요?

Can I try it on?

15 *Do you have this in another size?*

Do you have this in another size? 이거 다른 사이즈도 있나요?

Do you have this in another size?

16 *That's too expensive.*

That's too expensive. 너무 비싸요.

That's too expensive.

날씨 관련 표현하기

17 *How's the weather today?*

How's the weather today? 오늘 날씨 어때요?

How's the weather today?

18 *It's sunny and warm.*

It's sunny and warm. 날씨가 맑고 따뜻해요.

It's sunny and warm.

19 *It looks like it's going to rain.*

It looks like it's going to rain. 비가 올 것 같아요.

It looks like it's going to rain.

20 *It's really cold outside.*

It's really cold outside. 밖이 정말 추워요.

It's really cold outside.

100문장으로 끝내는 정말 쉬운 영어 필기체
자유롭게 적어보기

특별한 날 편지 쓰기 20

감사 편지

1
Thank you for your kindness.

Thank you for your kindness. 당신의 친절에 감사드립니다.

Thank you for your kindness.

2
I really appreciate your help.

I really appreciate your help. 도움을 정말 감사하게 생각해요.

I really appreciate your help.

3
You made my day.

You made my day. 당신 덕분에 하루가 행복했어요.

You made my day.

4
I'm grateful for everything.

I'm grateful for everything. 모든 것에 감사드려요.

I'm grateful for everything.

여행 중 편지

5

Greetings from Paris!

Greetings from Paris! 파리에서 인사드려요!

6

I wish you were here.

I wish you were here. 당신이 여기 있으면 좋겠어요.

7

I'm having a wonderful time.

I'm having a wonderful time. 저는 멋진 시간을 보내고 있어요.

8

I'll tell you all about it when I return.

I'll tell you all about it when I return. 돌아가면 다 이야기해 줄게요.

사과 편지

9

I'm sorry for what I said.

I'm sorry for what I said. 내가 했던 말에 대해 미안해요.

I'm sorry for what I said.

10

Please forgive me.

Please forgive me. 제발 저를 용서해 주세요.

Please forgive me.

11

I didn't mean to hurt you.

I didn't mean to hurt you. 당신을 상처 줄 의도는 없었어요.

I didn't mean to hurt you.

12

I hope we can make things right.

I hope we can make things right. 우리가 잘 해결할 수 있기를 바라요.

I hope we can make things right.

졸업 축하 편지

13 *Congratulations on your graduation!*
Congratulations on your graduation! 졸업을 축하해요!

Congratulations on your graduation!

14 *Wishing you success in your next journey.*
Wishing you success in your next journey. 앞으로의 여정에서 성공을 기원합니다.

Wishing you success in your next journey.

15 *The future is bright for you.*
The future is bright for you. 당신의 미래는 밝습니다.

The future is bright for you.

16 *Your hard work has paid off.*
Your hard work has paid off. 당신의 노력은 결실을 맺었어요.

Your hard work has paid off.

시험 / 도전 응원 편지

17 *Good luck on your exam!*

Good luck on your exam! 시험 잘 보세요!

18 *I believe in you.*

I believe in you. 나는 당신을 믿어요.

19 *Do your best and don't give up.*

Do your best and don't give up. 최선을 다하고 포기하지 마세요.

20 *I'm cheering for your success.*

I'm cheering for your success. 당신의 성공을 응원해요.

100문장으로 끝내는 정말 쉬운 영어 필기체
자유롭게 적어보기

영어 일기 필수 문장 20

가족에 대한 표현

1 *I had dinner with my family.*
I had dinner with my family. 가족과 저녁을 먹었다.

2 *My parents always support me.*
My parents always support me. 부모님은 늘 나를 응원해 주신다.

3 *I talked with my sister for a long time.*
I talked with my sister for a long time. 여동생과 오래 이야기를 나눴다.

4 *I miss my family when I'm away.*
I miss my family when I'm away. 집을 떠나면 가족이 그립다.

학교에 대한 표현

5 *I have too much homework today.*

I have too much homework today. 오늘 숙제가 너무 많다.

I have too much homework today.

6 *I learned something new in class.*

I learned something new in class. 수업에서 새로운 것을 배웠다.

I learned something new in class.

7 *I'm worried about the test tomorrow.*

I'm worried about the test tomorrow. 내일 시험이 걱정된다.

I'm worried about the test tomorrow.

8 *I can't wait for the school vacation.*

I can't wait for the school vacation. 방학이 너무 기다려진다.

I can't wait for the school vacation.

꿈 / 미래 표현

9 *I dream of becoming a writer.*

I dream of becoming a writer. 나는 작가가 되는 것이 꿈이다.

10 *My goal is to travel the world.*

My goal is to travel the world. 내 목표는 세계 여행을 하는 것이다.

11 *I hope my future will be bright.*

I hope my future will be bright. 내 미래가 밝기를 바란다.

12 *I want to do something meaningful.*

I want to do something meaningful. 의미 있는 일을 하고 싶다.

여행 / 나들이에 대한 표현

13 *I went to the beach today.*

I went to the beach today. 오늘은 해변에 갔다.

14 *Traveling makes me happy.*

Traveling makes me happy. 여행은 나를 행복하게 만든다.

15 *I took many photos on my trip.*

I took many photos on my trip. 여행에서 사진을 많이 찍었다.

16 *I want to visit new places.*

I want to visit new places. 새로운 곳들을 방문하고 싶다.

특별한 하루 표현

17 *Today is my birthday.*

Today is my birthday. 오늘은 내 생일이다.

Today is my birthday

18 *I received a wonderful gift.*

I received a wonderful gift. 멋진 선물을 받았다.

I received a wonderful gift.

19 *It was an unforgettable day.*

It was an unforgettable day. 잊을 수 없는 하루였다.

It was an unforgettable day

20 *I celebrated with my family.*

I celebrated with my family. 가족과 함께 축하했다.

I celebrated with my family

100문장으로 끝내는 정말 쉬운 영어 필기체
자유롭게 적어보기

속담 및 격언 명문장 20

노력에 대하여

1
No pain, no gain.

No pain, no gain. 고생 없이는 얻는 것도 없다.

2
Practice makes perfect.

Practice makes perfect. 연습이 완벽을 만든다.

3
Rome wasn't built in a day.

Rome wasn't built in a day. 로마는 하루아침에 이루어진 게 아니다.

4
Hard work pays off.

Hard work pays off. 노력은 결국 보상받는다.

시간에 대하여

5

Time is money.

Time is money. 시간은 돈이다.

6

Better late than never.

Better late than never. 늦더라도 안 하는 것보다는 낫다.

7

Lost time is never found again.

Lost time is never found again. 잃어버린 시간은 다시 찾을 수 없다.

8

Tomorrow is another day.

Tomorrow is another day. 내일은 또 다른 날이다.

건강에 대하여

9 *Health is wealth.*

Health is wealth. 건강이 곧 재산이다.

10 *An apple a day keeps the doctor away.*

An apple a day keeps the doctor away. 하루 한 알의 사과는 의사를 멀리한다.

11 *A sound mind in a sound body.*

A sound mind in a sound body. 건전한 정신은 건전한 육체에 깃든다.

12 *Prevention is better than cure.*

Prevention is better than cure. 치료보다 예방이 낫다.

운 / 기회에 대하여

13 *Opportunity knocks but once.*
Opportunity knocks but once. 기회는 한 번만 온다.

Opportunity knocks but once.

14 *Luck favors the prepared mind.*
Luck favors the prepared mind. 운은 준비된 마음을 따른다.

Luck favors the prepared mind.

15 *Make hay while the sun shines.*
Make hay while the sun shines. 해가 비칠 때 건초를 만들어라.

Make hay while the sun shines.

16 *Strike while the iron is hot.*
Strike while the iron is hot. 쇠뿔도 단김에 빼라.

Strike while the iron is hot.

성공 / 실패에 대하여

17 *Failure is the mother of success.*
Failure is the mother of success. 실패는 성공의 어머니다.

18 *Success doesn't come overnight.*
Success doesn't come overnight. 성공은 하룻밤 사이에 오지 않는다.

19 *Learn from your mistakes.*
Learn from your mistakes. 실수에서 배워라.

20 *Every failure is a step to success.*
Every failure is a step to success. 모든 실패는 성공으로 가는 한 걸음이다.

100문장으로 끝내는 정말 쉬운 영어 필기체
자유롭게 적어보기

명사들의 명언 쓰기 20

스포츠인

1
Just play. Have fun. Enjoy the game.
Just play. Have fun. Enjoy the game. 그냥 뛰어라. 즐겨라. 경기를 만끽하라.

Michael Jordan(마이클 조던)

2
Hard work beats talent when talent doesn't work hard.
Hard work beats talent when talent doesn't work hard. 재능이 노력하지 않을 때, 노력은 재능을 이긴다.

Tim Notke(팀 노케)

3
Champions keep playing until they get it right.
Champions keep playing until they get it right. 챔피언은 제대로 될 때까지 계속 시도한다.

Billie Jean King(빌리 진 킹)

4
Success is no accident.
Success is no accident. 성공은 우연이 아니다.

Pelé(펠레)

철학자

5 *The unexamined life is not worth living.*

The unexamined life is not worth living. 성찰하지 않는 삶은 살 가치가 없다.

Socrates(소크라테스)

The unexamined life is not worth living.

6 *Happiness depends upon ourselves.*

Happiness depends upon ourselves. 행복은 우리 자신에게 달려 있다.

Aristotle(아리스토텔레스)

Happiness depends upon ourselves.

7 *Man is the measure of all things.*

Man is the measure of all things. 인간은 만물의 척도다.

Protagoras(프로타고라스)

Man is the measure of all things.

8 *I think, therefore I am.*

I think, therefore I am. 나는 생각한다, 고로 존재한다.

René Descartes(르네 데카르트)

I think, therefore I am.

지도자

9 *Be the change that you wish to see in the world.*

Be the change that you wish to see in the world. 당신이 세상에서 보고 싶은 변화가 되라.

Mahatma Gandhi(마하트마 간디)

Be the change that you wish to see in the world.

10 *Injustice anywhere is a threat to justice everywhere.*

Injustice anywhere is a threat to justice everywhere. 어디서든 불의는 모든 곳의 정의를 위협한다.

Martin Luther King Jr(마틴 루터 킹)

Injustice anywhere is a threat to justice everywhere.

11 *I never lose. I either win or learn.*

I never lose. I either win or learn. 나는 결코 지지 않는다. 이기거나 배우거나 둘 중 하나다.

Nelson Mandela(넬슨 만델라)

I never lose. I either win or learn.

12 *Give me liberty, or give me death!*

Give me liberty, or give me death! 자유가 아니면 죽음을 달라!

Patrick Henry(패트릭 헨리)

Give me liberty, or give me death!

시인

13 *Fill your paper with the breathings of your heart.*

Fill your paper with the breathings of your heart. 당신의 종이를 마음의 숨결로 채워라.

William Wordsworth(윌리엄 워즈워스)

Fill your paper with the breathings of your heart.

14 *The only way to have a friend is to be one.*

The only way to have a friend is to be one. 친구를 얻는 유일한 방법은 먼저 친구가 되는 것이다.

Ralph Waldo Emerson(랄프 월도 에머슨)

The only way to have a friend is to be one.

15 *Forever is composed of nows.*

Forever is composed of nows. 영원은 지금이라는 순간들로 이루어져 있다.

Emily Dickinson(에밀리 디킨슨)

Forever is composed of nows.

16 *Nothing will work unless you do.*

Nothing will work unless you do. 당신이 움직이지 않으면 어떤 것도 작동하지 않는다.

Maya Angelou(마야 안젤루)

Nothing will work unless you do.

발명가

17

There is no substitute for hard work.

There is no substitute for hard work. 노력에는 대체물이 없다.

Thomas Edison(토머스 에디슨)

18

When one door closes, another opens.

When one door closes, another opens. 하나의 문이 닫히면, 다른 문이 열린다.

Alexander Graham Bell(알렉산더 그레이엄 벨)

19

The present is theirs; the future, for which I really worked, is mine.

The present is theirs; the future, for which I really worked, is mine. 현재는 그들의 것이고, 내가 진정으로 노력한 미래는 나의 것이다.

Nikola Tesla(니콜라 테슬라)

20

Imagination is more important than knowledge.

Imagination is more important than knowledge. 상상력이 지식보다 더 중요하다.

Albert Einstein(알버트 아이슈타인)

100문장으로 끝내는 정말 쉬운 영어 필기체
자유롭게 적어보기

Rome wasn't built in a day.

100문장으로 끝내는 정말 쉬운 영어 필기체

Step 3

문학작품 써보기

The Wizard of Oz
오즈의 마법사 1

- Dorothy lived in Kansas with her uncle and aunt.
- One day a big cyclone carried her house to the Land of Oz.
- She met a Scarecrow, a Tin Woodman, and a Lion.
- They all wanted something: brains, a heart, and courage.
- At the Emerald City they found the Wizard, but he was only an ordinary man.
- In the end, Dorothy tapped her silver shoes and went back home, saying, "There's no place like home."

- Dorothy lived in Kansas with her uncle and aunt.
- One day a big cyclone carried her house to the Land of Oz.
- She met a Scarecrow, a Tin Woodman, and a Lion.
- They all wanted something: brains, a heart, and courage.
- At the Emerald City they found the Wizard, but he was only an ordinary man.
- In the end, Dorothy tapped her silver shoes and went back home, saying, "There's no place like home."

- 도로시는 캔자스에서 삼촌과 숙모와 살았다.
- 어느 날 큰 회오리바람이 집을 오즈의 나라로 데려갔다.
- 그녀는 허수아비, 양철 나무꾼, 사자를 만났다.
- 그들은 두뇌, 마음, 용기를 원했다.
- 에메랄드 시티에서 그들은 마법사를 만났지만, 그는 평범한 사람이었다.
- 결국 도로시는 은 구두를 두드려 집으로 돌아가며 말했다. "집만 한 곳은 없어."

한 번 쓰기

두 번 쓰기

The Wizard of Oz
오즈의 마법사 2

- Dorothy walked along the yellow brick road.
- She saw a Scarecrow standing in a field.
- The Scarecrow could talk and asked to join her.
- "I want some brains," he said.
- Dorothy smiled and said he could come.
- They became good friends on the way.
- Together, they walked toward the Emerald City.

- Dorothy walked along the yellow brick road.
- She saw a Scarecrow standing in a field.
- The Scarecrow could talk and asked to join her.
- "I want some brains," he said.
- Dorothy smiled and said he could come.
- They became good friends on the way.
- Together, they walked toward the Emerald City.

- 도로시는 노란 벽돌길을 걸었다.
- 들판에 서 있는 허수아비를 보았다.
- 허수아비는 말을 할 수 있었고 그녀에게 함께 가자고 했다.
- "나는 두뇌가 필요해," 그가 말했다.
- 도로시는 웃으며 같이 가자고 말했다.
- 그들은 길에서 좋은 친구가 되었다.
- 함께 에메랄드 시티로 걸어갔다.

한 번 쓰기

두 번 쓰기

The Wizard of Oz
오즈의 마법사 3

- Dorothy and the Scarecrow walked into the forest.
- There they heard a strange sound of metal.
- They found a Tin Woodman standing still.
- He was rusty and could not move.
- They oiled his joints with kindness.
- The Tin Woodman began to move again.
- "I want a heart," he said, and he joined the journey.

- Dorothy and the Scarecrow walked into the forest.
- There they heard a strange sound of metal.
- They found a Tin Woodman standing still.
- He was rusty and could not move.
- They oiled his joints with kindness.
- The Tin Woodman began to move again.
- "I want a heart," he said, and he joined the journey.

- 도로시와 허수아비는 숲으로 들어갔다.
- 거기서 금속 소리를 들었다.
- 그들은 멈춰 서 있는 양철 나무꾼을 발견했다.
- 그는 녹슬어 움직이지 못했다.
- 그들은 친절히 그의 관절에 기름을 발라주었다.
- 양철 나무꾼은 다시 움직이기 시작했다.
- "나는 마음이 필요해," 그가 말하며 여정에 합류했다.

한 번 쓰기

두 번 쓰기

The Wizard of Oz
오즈의 마법사 4

- On the road, a great Lion jumped out.
- He roared loudly at Dorothy and her friends.
- Toto barked bravely at the Lion.
- Dorothy told the Lion not to be cruel.
- The Lion began to cry sadly.
- "I am a coward. I want courage," he said.
- The friends comforted him, and he joined them.

- On the road, a great Lion jumped out.
- He roared loudly at Dorothy and her friends.
- Toto barked bravely at the Lion.
- Dorothy told the Lion not to be cruel.
- The Lion began to cry sadly.
- "I am a coward. I want courage," he said.
- The friends comforted him, and he joined them.

- 길 위에서 큰 사자가 뛰어나왔다.
- 그는 도로시와 친구들에게 크게 포효했다.
- 토토가 용감하게 사자에게 짖었다.
- 도로시는 사자에게 잔인하지 말라고 말했다.
- 사자는 슬프게 울기 시작했다.
- "나는 겁쟁이야. 용기가 필요해," 그가 말했다.
- 친구들이 그를 위로했고, 사자는 합류했다.

한 번 쓰기

두 번 쓰기

The Wizard of Oz
오즈의 마법사 5

- *Dorothy and her friends reached the Emerald City.*
- *The Wizard looked powerful and mysterious.*
- *They bowed before him with respect.*
- *Later, they found a small man behind a curtain.*
- *"I am Oz, the Great and Terrible," he said.*
- *They were shocked that he had no real magic.*
- *But they learned that they already had brains, heart, and courage.*

- Dorothy and her friends reached the Emerald City.
- The Wizard looked powerful and mysterious.
- They bowed before him with respect.
- Later, they found a small man behind a curtain.
- "I am Oz, the Great and Terrible," he said.
- They were shocked that he had no real magic.
- But they learned that they already had brains, heart, and courage.

- 도로시와 친구들은 에메랄드 시티에 도착했다.
- 마법사는 강력하고 신비해 보였다.
- 그들은 그 앞에 존경을 담아 절했다.
- 나중에 그들은 커튼 뒤에 있는 작은 남자를 발견했다.
- "나는 위대하고 두려운 오즈다," 그가 말했다.
- 그들은 그에게 진짜 마법이 없다는 사실에 충격받았다.
- 그러나 그들은 이미 두뇌와 마음, 용기를 지니고 있음을 깨달았다.

한 번 쓰기

두 번 쓰기

Aesop's Fable – The Tortoise and the Hare
이솝 우화 - 토끼와 거북이

- The Hare laughed at the slow Tortoise.
- He said the Tortoise could never win a race.
- The Tortoise challenged him to try.
- They started running, and the Hare ran very fast.
- The Hare stopped to rest under a tree and fell asleep.
- The Tortoise walked slowly but never stopped.
- At last, the Tortoise reached the finish line first.

- The Hare laughed at the slow Tortoise.
- He said the Tortoise could never win a race.
- The Tortoise challenged him to try.
- They started running, and the Hare ran very fast.
- The Hare stopped to rest under a tree and fell asleep.
- The Tortoise walked slowly but never stopped.
- At last, the Tortoise reached the finish line first.

- 토끼는 느린 거북이를 비웃었다.
- 그는 거북이가 결코 경주에서 이길 수 없다고 말했다.
- 거북이는 시합을 하자고 도전했다.
- 그들은 달리기를 시작했고, 토끼는 매우 빨리 달렸다.
- 토끼는 나무 아래서 쉬다 잠이 들었다.
- 거북이는 천천히 걸었지만 멈추지 않았다.
- 마침내 거북이가 결승선에 먼저 도착했다.

한 번 쓰기

두 번 쓰기

Aesop's Fable – The Lion and the Mouse

이솝 우화 - 사자와 생쥐

- One day a Lion caught a little Mouse.
- The Mouse begged for his life.
- "Please let me go. I will help you someday," he said.
- The Lion laughed but set him free.
- Later, the Lion was caught in a hunter's net.
- The Mouse came and chewed the ropes.
- The Lion was free and thanked the Mouse.

- One day a Lion caught a little Mouse.
- The Mouse begged for his life.
- "Please let me go. I will help you someday," he said.
- The Lion laughed but set him free.
- Later, the Lion was caught in a hunter's net.
- The Mouse came and chewed the ropes.
- The Lion was free and thanked the Mouse.

- 어느 날 사자가 작은 생쥐를 잡았다.
- 생쥐는 목숨을 구해 달라고 애원했다.
- "제발 날 놓아 줘. 언젠가 내가 도와줄게," 그가 말했다.
- 사자는 웃었지만 그를 풀어주었다.
- 나중에 사자가 사냥꾼의 그물에 잡혔다.
- 생쥐가 와서 줄을 갉아 먹었다.
- 사자는 자유로워졌고 생쥐에게 감사했다.

한 번 쓰기

두 번 쓰기

Aesop's Fable – The Fox and the Grapes

이솝 우화 - 여우와 신 포도

- A Fox saw some grapes hanging high on a vine.
- He wanted to eat them very much.
- He jumped and tried to reach the grapes.
- He jumped again but still could not get them.
- He tried many times but always failed.
- The grapes were too high for him.
- At last, he walked away saying, "Those grapes are sour."

- A Fox saw some grapes hanging high on a vine.
- He wanted to eat them very much.
- He jumped and tried to reach the grapes.
- He jumped again but still could not get them.
- He tried many times but always failed.
- The grapes were too high for him.
- At last, he walked away saying, "Those grapes are sour."

- 여우가 덩굴에 높이 매달린 포도를 보았다.
- 그는 그것을 무척 먹고 싶었다.
- 여우는 뛰어올라 포도를 잡으려 했다.
- 그는 다시 뛰었지만 여전히 닿지 못했다.
- 여러 번 시도했지만 항상 실패했다.
- 포도는 그에게 너무 높이 있었다.
- 마침내 그는 "저 포도는 시다"라고 말하며 떠났다.

한 번 쓰기

두 번 쓰기

Thank you for always being there for me.
Thank you for always being there for me. 나를 항상 곁에서 응원해줘서 고마워.

Wishing you a heart full of happiness and love.
Wishing you a heart full of happiness and love. 당신의 마음이 행복과 사랑으로 가득하길 바래요.

You make my days brighter just by being in them.
You make my days brighter just by being in them. 당신 덕분에 내 하루가 더 빛나요.

I'm so lucky to have a friend like you.
I'm so lucky to have a friend like you. 당신 같은 친구가 있어서 정말 행운이에요.

May your dreams bloom like spring flowers.
May your dreams bloom like spring flowers. 당신의 꿈이 봄꽃처럼 활짝 피어나길 바래요.

Merry Christmas and may your new year sparkle with joy!
Merry Christmas and may your new year sparkle with joy! 메리 크리스마스, 새해에는 기쁨이 반짝이길!

Your kindness means the world to me.
Your kindness means the world to me. 당신의 따뜻함이 제게 큰 힘이 돼요.

Just a little note to say you're amazing.
Just a little note to say you're amazing. 당신은 정말 멋지다는 말을 꼭 전하고 싶었어요.

With all my love, now and always.
With all my love, now and always. 언제나, 변함없이 진심을 담아.